A GOAT FROM A DISTANCE

A GOAT FROM A DISTANCE

poems

Jennifer Moss

Dream Horse Press
Aptos, California

Dream Horse Press
Post Office Box 670 Warrenton, Oregon 97146

Printed in the United States of America
Published in 2017 by Dream Horse Press

ISBN 978-1-935716-44-0

Cover artwork:
Spoken Word
by Karine Swenson
karineswenson.com

CONTENTS

For my mother and father

FIELD

Nothing about her
let me think
she wasn't
a real
goat until I
saw the straw
hat behind
her hips she
said: "I see you're
a goat too."

I

THE PUPPET

In him everything is waiting:
unheated air, belief in solitude,
belief in steps into the man
living in the woman.
The red felt tongue is out of time
and slack between the lips.
I make my hand the rigor in his heart;
he's trying to tell the other, as they meet,
"I knew nothing, I knew nothing."
Let's turn the figure upside down
and look into his head. When we invent
his mind we give him memory;
at first he's hesitant, but then he plays with it.
He's in a dream and feels the rhythm beating there:
blue caves-into blue, caves-into white,
to the sunlight in a room,
where he sits down on a chair and sees
the crooked leaves piled in ditches.
It's the unhealthy smell of yellow trees
that holds on in his throat.
And it's here he stays, waiting
with a comic look of worry
at the corners of his mouth. It all
appeals to his mind like the first long day
of loneliness, when the hand will move outside,
and he forgets which way he came.

A MAN HAD A BIRD

that clutched my finger
and moved its voice
over bits of song.
It was this man's idea
to teach his bird
the funny tunes he knew.
Its throat,
in the puffed-up
down, was a thin
and knotty cord.
Its feathers were gray
and did not smell
of anything.
Its eyes were black
or dark brown
and their surface
held the room
in miniature. It seemed
to have a reason
for its singing
and stopping
that had less to do
with pleasure
than with exactitude
in sound.
It took the silly notes
the man gave out
and gave them back to him.
I think he liked
to hear his songs

arrange the bird's new memory.
I think he loved the bird
the way a small boy
loves himself
inside his doll.
He dangled shiny strings
of metal beads
and the bird
pulled violently at them.
He laughed
and shut them in a drawer,
then held a piece of
mirror up to the bird's
face: he said
this always worked
to make it sing again.

IN MAMMAL HALL

What keeps me staring
is the absence of this zebra,
looking so present.
When I watch without blinking,
it looks like he's breathing.
Getting closer I see the place
where they slit him open,
the narrow, stitched seam in the hide
running along the belly, up the legs,
breast, neck, to lower jaw.
I meet his glass eye with my eye.

Because he's empty, this zebra is mine.
I fill his body with my mind
to give my thought a shape.
In the painted desert scene behind him
other zebras graze and nap,
but he's not interested in them.
He's standing on his wooden mount
staring through the glass
as if some sharp urge had pierced his heart
and frozen him in space.
The border of the brain turns cold.

THE PET

The door knobs shimmer.
Tears can trickle somewhere leaving their salt skins.
I am a lover of light,
my claws click in the cool halls.

The boy sleeps alone tonight in his long nursery;
in the night the pulse stops in his wrists and groin.
His lips are sour, he has left his mind
like a flower found on a walk and carried

but put back on the path.
I'm not afraid of domestics with their dull teeth,
there is sugar in the rice,
bicycles are ringing with pleasure,

over the bed purple drapes across blue.
Here's what I might choose:
robes and rubber balls, soldiers, upholstery,
I show the tall woman I'm not afraid

of loud talk in salons,
not of the marble green bust of my sister.
They are all naughty and free
to give nothing or everything,

they kiss my pink tongue.
Workers are loading the linens and opening vents,
they've pinned a white ribbon into my hair,
wiped up my chin, orders are growing below;

here comes sunlight on the silk sheets,
shit in the ruffles,
someone is shrieking his name, I know they have maps,
but they don't come back, they don't use them.

AN ANTHILL

So red and black
it's almost purple,
the anthill looks raw,
looks like it hurts.
The ants have been forming it
from dead needles and twigs
for as long as I
remember. It crackles
nearly inaudibly.
It is a place to watch
thought in action,
each argument
being pursued with
purpose and tenacity
to build this one idea,
this symbol,
this thing—
vivid with meaning,
historical, intricate,
protecting a truth
at the heart.
Four feet tall
and wider at the base
it engulfs
the slim trunk of a fir.
How clearly into
the hill's logic
these ants can see:
their ferocious
attacking and quick

fixing when unexpectedly
it is disturbed—
by a stick, or,
like when I was
a child, a body
falling into it.
They believe in
one ideology,
a fierce morality.
Their hill
is the shape of vigilance.
The uncertainty
in one moment
can scare you stiff:
they're constructing proofs
against it.

THE JAR

(The Jar)

On the back mountain
with a pick-ax and drill
I dug to the center
and filled my bag
with chunks of silica,
then brought them home
and smashed them into powder,
sprinkled in some soda-lime,
and put the mixture in a fire.
I had a thought, the thought knew me
when I pulled my steel pipe from flames.
I spun the molten mass I'd made
then gathered more; the glass turned red.
Through the hollow pipe
I blew a steady stream
and saw the jar begin.
It watched me from the pipe's end.

(Now)

Now take the jar away
it has a gaping mouth
and cries
fill it with gravel
water or your breath
that fogs
screw on the lid

(just keep a steady hand)
and hide it far
across the river
(destroy the bridge)
behind the hills
put it completely
out of mind.

(Jar Dream #1)

When the jar returns to me,
I am the mother it loved.
When I feed it my breast, it turns blue.
I thought about the clouds the jar came from.
I thought about the rain
falling out of my face into the river.
The river was silent
because I was the father.
I was always the father.
Then I picked up the jar and hid it.

(The Life of the Jar)

The jar shook and turned
and sniffed the wind.
It smiled, put its lips
to the thrashing river
and sucked it dry.

It chewed the river bed
for days and nights, alone,
a heartbeat in its ears.
I stayed just out of sight
and watched it, half with pride,
half with aching fear.
The sun struck its glass
and spread a rainbow in its ravaged wake.
When it reached the ocean's mouth
it called for me and cried
and my chest filled up with love.

(Jar Dream #2)

What are they doing?

—Floating inside the jar.

Who shapes and turns them?

—Carbon makes them glow.

Who cradles their ribs?

—They cradle each other.

Who sits behind their eyes? Who directs?

—The black sky pulls them.

Do they see the tree line filled with breath?

—They search for their reflections.

Do they feel the lightning snap?

—They look, then look away.

Are they hoping we will laugh?

—They play with sticks and bones.

Do they love us? Do they call us?

—They crack and break in two.

What happens to them then?

—What happens to you?

(The Jar's End)

Jar I never knew you
your jaws
were too wide
stop waiting
with an open
mouth let me out
of sight

your everywhere eye
Jar stop
waiting
don't make me stop you

(The Jar Sits Inside of You)

The jar sits inside of you

like a first desire for symmetry

like an inhale

like a kiss in the middle of the forehead

like a root

like a brown root

twisted around and around itself

like a held breath

like possible snowfall

like a slap

like rocks closing themselves

like one year like two

like the bones of a paw

or a spider's husk

the brain of an ant underground

like the sun pressing into grass

like someone lifting you slowly

like a pink mouth

a row of hard teeth

like a voice opening up one note

like a green tree filling the window

like an exhale

like the birds at night

(the jar sits inside of you)

DUCKING IN AND OUT OF SHADOWS

Ducking in and out of shadows, I thought:
the sun does always make me lengthen.

I thought it as a form of meditation.
As a labyrinthine message to something that watches.

I felt the watcher but was afraid to speak.
So I drew it closer with my fear.

And what I feared came.
Alone over the rocks.

A goat from a distance walking toward me.
I felt a debt to the goat

walking from that distance.
The broken branches

there in the wide clearing.
A silver thread blowing in and out of visibility.

The goat's womanish head bobbed up and down.
When she reached me, one yellow eye turned toward the sun.

The goat was a body filled with disease.
I put a rope around her neck

and led her to a treeless field.
And hit her with a switch.

Her legs shattered when she sprang.
The goat lay in the dust,

her bloated belly heaving.
Under my shadow, lengthening.

Which became longer the deeper she breathed.
Which grew great and covered us both.

I shook and cried under the sky over the goat.
And this kept us alive.

THREE OCTOPI

Three octopi on a platter of ice.
Six aristocratic eyes.
Raise the cutlery and slice.

—How was your life?
—Green and wide.
—Will the sky die? Will it break like glass?
—We are just three octopi.

Three octopi on a platter of ice.
They are glistening, preposterous and smooth.
Through the windows the mountains are precise.

MAKING THE CENTAUR

It seemed the horse arrived with the wind,
and the white flash of his eyes suggested

thoughts that were three-fourths fear,
the tingle in his nerves racing toward injury.

In a sudden kick and burst through the fields
he was chased by earth's symbols,

all beauty turned hostile.
A spiral in the wild sky noosed him,

terror cinching him up hoof to head,
and the clouds appeared, after, always arranged by pain.

His will now tangled fiercely with yours,
it rains all day on the tin roof,

foam smeared over his flanks,
his mental heat phantoming.

All day his voice twisting in the air.
Then, toward night, there is the break:

the deep restraint you recognize in the rope,
some strength the horse keeps in darkness.

A new creature rises up between you.

II

ANOTHER AGE

Then the snake came
out of the hum
of an ice age;
a snake carving
through the ice
to come to
the end of an age,
to the beginning
of a new snake-head
and spine: blood
expanding, a pulse
quickening, then
the red tongue
touching air,
a spasm of muscle
over rocks
and debris,
dividing with
his length the world
into right and
left, the world's
particulars
under his body,
the world's language
forming tight inside
his brain. The language
was ponderous
requiring shadows,
the snake acknowledged
the sun, while in

a fugue his days
and nights repeated
winding on a vine,
each thing before him
transformed into
possibility,
each thing behind
into philosophy,
until he had made
for himself a mortal
space and lived there.
What shall we do
with the snake when
we find him, his
concentration
severe in the leaves?
Hold out a stick
and watch him slowly
wrap himself around it.
Bring him closer.
Do you hear
your mind begin
to speak to you?
Lift the long
coil of matter
up to the light:
the vivid head
unintelligible,
the still eye fixed
on you, and another
age begins.

THE PADDOCK

That day Mrs. Semple told me not to cross the road;
she said I shouldn't look beyond the ditch
of brittle grass, beyond the low stone wall

and climb, the way I always did,
along the peeling paddock fence.
Her face remained inscrutable with lines.

She wore a pair of dusty jeans tucked into
long, black rubber boots, and kept her right hand
on her hip. She turned and walked away.

It was not so much my curiosity as need
to know. I don't remember if I'd seen it once before,
but when I crossed the road and looked

over the fence, death didn't startle me.
But it was strange—that pony I'd seen every day,
lying in the dust in such a crooked shape.

Her left hooves stuck into the buzzing air,
her neck arched back and set the big head
stiffly on the ground. It was a kind of

parody of sleep. But it was more than that:
her body didn't fit to movement
anymore and it had swelled with something else.

The parted lips exposed the brown, streaked teeth.
The smooth, black coat absorbed the beating sun.
She was more comprehensible than she had ever been.

BIRTHDAY PARTY

Songs are sweaty. We wear hats
and then we don't.

The rabbit by the stump is filled with worms.
I tell my brother I'm the monster.

Trees eat music; he runs
out to the open field, under an airplane line

until I step into the sun.
He wears pointy shoes that glitter, grass sticks in his socks,

I circle him and circle tighter,
I sing, "dead men, dead men."

Before I change back into myself
I make him say he loves the monster.

WEATHER, SHAPE, DISTANCE

(The clouds were a colorless semaphore.)
A panache of birds in the oaks and the air
like an incessant voice beside me, then I felt
the catch in my throat become girlish.

A panache of birds in the oaks and the air
hovering over the ruptures of green. It made
the catch in my throat become girlish.
One memory returned, crow-like,

hovering over the ruptures of green. It made
the surface of the pasture shimmer.
One memory returned, crow-like,
eating through the excess where I saw

the surface of the pasture shimmer.
(The clouds removed the sky.) So the memory became conscious,
eating through the excess where I saw
its progress ended in a face, like an apparition.

(The clouds removed the sky.) So the memory became conscious
of my seeing it, and through the gaping hole
its progress ended in a face, like an apparition,
all at once adult, inconsolable, aware

of my seeing it, and through the gaping hole
it gaped back. I felt I was being followed,
all at once adult, inconsolable, aware.
(The warning of rain in a rumble above.)

It gaped back. I felt I was being followed.
Then I knew it was in me—my father's face, crying
(the warning of rain in a rumble above),
turning to face me, pulling me toward him.

Then I knew it was in me—my father's face, crying
(the rain suddenly starting),
turning to face me, pulling me toward him,
shaking, saying, "you'll always be sad."

(The rain suddenly starting.)
Then hearing the voice—desolate, infectious,
shaking, saying, "you'll always be sad."
I tried to pat the face.

Then hearing the voice—desolate, infectious,
an ache in my thinking formed.
I tried to pat the face
but it was words swimming over the pasture.

An ache in my thinking formed.
I sat in the wet grass, explaining,
but it was words swimming over the pasture.
(The crows stood like holes in the trees.)

I sat in the wet grass, explaining,
while the fetid air thickened, wrapped around like a cape.
(The crows stood like holes in the trees.)
And I was left with myself

while the fetid air thickened, wrapped around like a cape.
The birds took flight calling, circling,
and I was left with myself,
feverish in the swollen back pasture.

The birds took flight calling, circling
like an incessant voice beside me, then I felt
feverish in the swollen back pasture.
(The clouds were a colorless semaphore.)

CLOUDS

I think clouds might euthanize me

they sound

like a gravel driveway
like someone
sipping broth

like a clock

ticking

inside them

everything is magnified
and drips

the color of spoons
that is how they taste

Being inside is like falling

in and out

of an overheard conversation

losing a thought
picking it up losing

it again you could try to shine a light

but you won't

find anything Clouds are like

a string of events
an argument you see

plates and bowls
parents' faces
high ceilings
they
don't last

not like clouds
Clouds

hang over houses

over people looking
out of windows

over trees and long ditches

and wasps
crawling in the eaves

Days get dark early in empty rooms

breath is

papery and loud
I might think about clouds

for a while
in a dark room

And then I'm asleep

FOR BECKY

(1965-1993)

The forest today
the forest I remember always when I sleep:
solitary snags where bodies gnaw into the wood's heart,
towering firs inspiring Death's head to present
itself once more as my own,
the sun ancestral, grave,
its chain laid along this path
I take through the trees,
through the dirt by a blistering
ant hill alive like an inconsolable brain
and I am that brain's dark thought,
shadow falling over it.
This is where as kids we played the kissing game,
where I whipped my pony's neck,
where we tried to make each other faint.
The wind covers bark and fallen wings,
parts of the once-living who never disappear
even in their shapelessness. My friend,
grown now, has lost her son and daughter,
she's high up in the trees searching through
each needle—she nearly sees them before shade
slants into her insomnia
and she remembers they're not lost after all
since she died with them.
Along the forest floor the sheen of fever
covers everything; she comes down without tears,
without anger at her husband shaking in the clouds
and digs a hole big enough to lie in.
Here is my sleep cracked open,

its roots growing through her eyes
locked on an invisible moon.
The roots spread and sew her body to this earth,
this forest I remember, always,
where again she leaves my sleep.

NIGHTFALL

The song between two birds acquires shadows
overlaid with shadows; as the song stops
it forces out the moon's dull blade.
Now thought reveals its side
from hell and leaves me in that hemisphere.
The trees outside are darkly furred.
The house is helpless, its objects filled with danger
like a nail through a wall that sees. Deep inside me
something has turned foul.
God, please don't dissolve.
I know how much a head can hold, its threads
tangle up eternity. I know the heart is packed with time.
I had a dream in which I dug one twisted
root from dirt and all my teeth fell out.
This body is not mine.

THE RAPTOR TONIGHT

The raptor is watching.
Call her and she'll shift in the trees.
In the meager moonlight over the road,
she's a slippery witness.
The raptor knows what you can't.
She'll wait for the cold stars to hit their high-notes.
She'll spread her wings over your eyes:
  Clumsy child, spooked by time,
  the thoughts you've called your own
  don't matter now.
Go for a ride, cling to her breast,
her feathers as smooth as falling.
It's like a second birth
to hold the hunter tight.
Call her (she'll take you tonight).

III

COW

In her expression
is some skepticism.

THE HOSTESS

It was all so clean.
It was somewhat bright.
There were chairs and a table, a couch.
When the shades were down
you could see the squares of the windows
in shadow behind them.
My throat was dry, unclearable.
The radiator made sounds like a reptile.
Outside it sounded like there may have been crows.
I said: "I'll be right back to butter the pork."
I made up some lists.
I looked at them often.
I felt myself becoming less and less
a person of some important scheme.
I wasn't sure if it was true.
I called the time.
The forecast was pleasant.
I didn't catch it all.
I was so calm.
I was rearranging the chairs.
I spread a tablecloth and set out glasses.
I looked at my reflection in a spoon.
Something about it struck me hilarious—
I thought of that headline: FACE ON MARS
IS TRYING TO TALK.
All of a sudden I was shuddering.
I presented the first course
and it was referred to throughout the season.

FIELDS

The calf across the drift of grass called us.
Through the fields we heard the wind
clatter on the metal sheds,
on the stiff, gray blades of windmills.
The fields were cold
and the sharp plants came up to our chins.
We sang, the dirt warmed,
we took off our jackets, rolled up our sleeves.
The cows across the fields
wound like a slow, chestnut ribbon.
Sentences uncoiled over the square acres turning silver,
our faces tilted into the odorless sun.
And the machines on the horizon looked like toy machines,
bright with sun.
And the cows across the fields in the feedlots
were bright with sun.
The distance pulled us forward.
The strict distance where we fastened down the land
in nervous sentences.
The sky was sharp and clear.
We moved between rows, male and female.
Sometimes the taste of herbicide.
Sometimes the scent of infection.
Sentences slipped into blithering.
The bloated cows looked like toy cows,
eating pharmaceuticals from the troughs.
We licked our hands where the cuts had opened.
Words slipped into heavy breathing.
Machines churned through the receptive stalks.
A Cessna flew over the hills.

Through the hybrids our heads moved against the blue
screen of sky and sounds of exhaust and lowing
turned through the air.

THE FOG REMEMBERED FEVER

Fever was like water,
restless and dreamy.
Water was the dreamy part of fever,
and fever sometimes flashed like water
breaking over rocks in the river.
It made everyone dizzy to watch from above
and worried to watch from close up.
And fever showed pleasure, like water, in clouds
and secret voices, in fortunes, prayers,
in the sky's sudden shaking, in a downpour,
a battering, a road washed out.
The rain hypnotized.
A man was thinking of a word—
but it was the wrong word.
He was thinking of a plan,
but it was a crooked plan.
He reached for a face—
it was a stranger's face.
Someone said no, but fever said yes,
follow the stranger.
And the stranger became a bird, a swift bird,
a golden bird hiding in rain.
O *golden bird* the man said, and meant it.
O *soul* he said, and felt it.
Fever said search.
So the man searched for the bird
(but it had gone).
He had seen it so clearly
(but he couldn't remember).
His head swam with rain.

He came to under lights.
All eyes were upon him.
What had he done?
He felt ashamed.
There was no rain.
There was no fever.
Everyone laughed, and soon the man laughed too.
They all shuffled out through fog
toward a clear day.
They forgot fever.

(But the fog remembered fever.
The fog in its silver shawl remembered
when it tip-toed, when it whispered a beloved's name,
when it felt beside itself and weightless.)

A NEEDLE PULLING A THREAD

A needle pulling
a thread through fabric

is improper when it moans.
Holding an egg

in a fist
is improper.

Holding an egg
improperly,

and saying in a voice
sharp like a pinecone,

"Here's your egg,"
will require everyone

to quietly shift their shoes
under the table.

The silence in teacups
that makes a deep hole

can be remedied with
the passing of sugar

and then inquiries.
Do not let the sugar

plop, which is improper.
Do not let your mouth

fall slack,
do not let your eyes

drift over others
as if they were sleeping dogs.

If you must keep one ear
on a needle, if

you hear each moan,
or if one moan becomes

louder, if all moans
suddenly are calling,

then you should concentrate
on the faces before you,

and if they seem "just fine"
you may subtly

excuse yourself to
let the water run.

A needle pulling
a thread through fabric

should not be heard, though
the needle is necessary,

the thread has always
been a thread and will be

forever, passing in
and out of the long robe

which is invisible
but taking shape,

and one day soon it will be proper
for you to slip it on,

return, and lie down
at the feet of your guests.

A SHIFT IN THE HEAD WIND

A shift in the head wind
inevitable sun bleaching the grass
my face is fixed with itches and threads
yesterday the clouds turned
Gothic and Goliath really
the ants on this planet are mute I'm a boy
moving my mouth with the lights off
I'm a girl with salt around my lips
moony moony Man-in-the-moon
I saw the land laid out in light
you made it all so blue a something fabulous
shining down I felt celestial
and tinsel grows out of
memory you left the sky

I've seen myself quite large before
and in the brothy river corpuscular trees
and the sound of scissors ripping through
the falling rain and
the reproduction of brain-work
in the waves

The Father's stress turns meteorological
please touch
me disinherited
bright-eyed and bushy-tailed
ever on the lookout I've caught the girl inside myself
and dressed her up with dayside
yes really spellbound in the day
come into electricity

"She didn't know what month it was
and this caused many questions"

My name is dot dot dot I'm sure there's
meaning in the pattern and the invisible
fills the visible shape of a face
in here quite desperately
out there bodies turn into gossip
and cloudy conversations in the open air

FROM SICKNESS

From sickness, what do you hear?

    The tick of a floorboard
    swelling in the heat.

How deep do you sleep in sickness?

    Words lose their cargo,
    their sounds float free,
    and we find them *interesting*.

        To the sparrows an ox sings
        I am a small ox
        walking in a dark field.

    In the funnel of ears
     In the doorway overheard
      In dizziness

What does sickness mean?

    To fear the Lord
    (God's full attention upon us)
    is sickness made meaningful.

        I will change.

    We look out from sickness
    and read the signs.
    The signs sit in everything.

They are true, but untranslatable.

What will be my end?
What is moving me?
Shall I walk through the field?

And the question over and over to myself:
who am I?

and the answer:
I am two: I and you

BEASTS FRAMED THE FIELD I

Beast there is sun on your red belly
You lick yourself clean
smooth your legs and chest
the ax of your heart chops
through the forest   no rest
You have grown around your teeth
and instantly your eyes tighten on a target
My dogs won't answer to their names
they run off in their thick coats
Why not love the Other
playing his violin
Beast you lived a hidden life
now go away to sniff and dig
let's see your talent for living

BEASTS FRAMED THE FIELD II
(a beast speaks)

There your egg-shaped head
lit from behind
Your force sits in a room
I don't think you've felt your solitude
as much as you will at my paws before we
crash over the fossil bed
Your glasses stare at that dark window you keep touching
and talking to   Through the window
I can look you clean in the face
see the vein jump in your neck
and the salt shining over your lip
Could it be you want to rub your head against mine
Do you want our fur to crackle
Do you want to dig a hole in the field
dig back to your red and black birth
with me chasing after
Do you want each twist toward mother to hurt
and do you want to do it again

BEASTS FRAMED THE FIELD III

Because I am a trapdoor, hallucinating,
things seem, then things end.
Behind a door a red beast fought:
terse, acid, electrical with fear.
(In my eyes I saw the beast's eyes
filled with death, like fluorescent lights).
What would we do without the accusing sky above our heads?
I put the innards there to please the sun.
From the house, smoke rises like seraphim.

BEASTS FRAMED THE FIELD IV

Beast to be your friend I'd gather the clouds swarming over the river
I'd play the horn of forgiveness all night
I'd plant a garden in your name
and we could drink our milk together
To be your friend I would stop my voice
be still as a stump
so you might finally lie down beside my lap
and lick my hand and look into my eyes
You are a good Beast and to be your friend
I'd like to see your eyes soften
and I'd like to see your eyes follow my gaze
I'd like to see your eyes fill with worry when I set my sights
on another and I'd like to see
your jealous eye look after me a tremble down your spine
I'd like to see you at my leg when I walk
I'd like to feed you from my hand the suffering inborn
disease of my blood
I'd like to make your home between my walls
I'd like to hear you speak tell me where I'm from
it's all gone underwater
I'd like to be your friend

BEASTS FRAMED THE FIELD V

(a beast speaks)

Then the ambush from all sides.
The joys of the fight for the field!
Among the joys were a branching wind
and skies rushing over startled skins.
When my teeth caught your thigh
you rattled for the first time like an alien.
Thrust through the swift grass, your features distended.
Your voice, enchanted, came to life.
Your days of misfortune ended.

THE TUNNEL

He lived his life in a tunnel,
and he dug.
This made his face pointy.
He was born, slipping down a red sky
like a cough that grows into
the sound of a river shifting in thunder.
And then—he opened his eyes—a tunnel.
Moving through the tunnel pressed his insides.
This was to let him know how heavy
it was, how true.
Truth in the tunnel was always understood through weight.
Sometimes he doubted,
but the tunnel showed him the way out of doubt,
it had a parallel way of being dark and light at one distance.
He left scratches on the tunnel's sides—
drawings of torture and suffering.
This gave him solace.
When a drawing was finished he wrote words:
"The one distance gives birth to the Name within,"
and, "Who in all his silence is infinite,
in truth he goes to the one distance."
He dug in the tunnel; this was courage.
He added up days using songs with hand-claps.
Making shadows on his heavy eyes,
the tunnel drove him, it was restless,
it wore him down like metal scrapings,
and he dug.
When he finally lay gasping,
the tunnel tightened around his chest.
Its damp, whetstone scent moved him like a memory.

A space far away in his mind opened up.

Later, the sound of another's digging filled the tunnel.

A ROYAL LOST KINGDOM

Head always hurt, hurt hard.
In lightning I felt smaller, the reverse
of river, I felt shaking like asking questions,
I felt burning like tin and different eyes
in the rain as in the sun. I felt
like an infancy fire through a greasy pane of glass,
like an unseen edge or the slimy meat of dinner when
light snarled through the forks and I was
calculated into like a math problem.
I saw the little god's arms motioning
in silver, delicate steam or spaces
in a lullaby, only now it's dead, though sometimes
it sprouts voices. I'm waiting for a doctor
to put a light on it, I feel like a royal lost kingdom and
sometimes just the speck of an edge, as I said,
and hidden for 1,000 years.

THE STORM

Where one mind stops,
another begins.

Where cutlery shines on plates,
a voice lowers.

One length of forgiveness,
round and round like a child's game
in the dust.

Outside, the rain formalizing.

When we leave we are replaced.

Shaky clouds in lightning,
my shadow alive on the floor.

Then the small passage for sleep.

How green and spidery the sky.

In its net, the dead bees of memory.

ARTHUR GANSON'S *MACHINE WITH WISHBONE*

The wishbone walks like a drunk man, or a baby,
each step teetering barely into the next.
Its legs are clasped with metal cuffs.
From the cuffs, two slender rods run back to
the machine—an elegant invention of five wire wheels,
the largest two, like toy carnival rides, turning above.
Delicate gears, sprockets, spokes and springs
whir with a ghostly precision.
The wishbone, its neck stunted, without a head,
has a bottomless innocence, so earnest and submissive
it makes us want to look away.
Far behind, the machine pushes it slowly,
like a silver dream guiding the bone's destiny.

PORTRAIT

What withdrew from us   What moved
away over the buildings where there was
an inch of sun in the heavy sky
then looking over we thought we knew
nothing of it   The ambulance turning
its quiet lights   radio static through
the wide-angle view
of a parking garage   At the top two policemen
standing near a man sitting
at the edge   their stillness long
On the street the crowd abuzz and a chant
jump   jump   laughter   someone said
he'd been up there two hours
still no action

                    *

What I thought by the darkening wall
three crows calling out suddenly
to work the air with complicity such musical
blank time   The linear ornamental flowers
in a box   I felt the life-span
and a fumbling   Ideas they
don't matter   Who knows
how to look at the person next to you
he is tight breath and blue beneath
the skin   The chains on the flagpoles squeak out
forgiveness   fast blink

                    *

There is a skywalk
people meet there in the rain
and sun asking for innocence
leave off go looking for the doorway
I saw one segment of cloud
turn green and spread   A man looking down
from above   a crowd looking up

*

What breath on the forehead
What anima   the crickets drown
Take away the buried thread
Take away the father knife
What river   take away the shine

*

You know he is going to die
sometime   everything does   The reddening
trees beat out sound with their elastic
branches and sugar   still the world depends on
him   wind dissolves in his veins
nothing exists by itself but now
he is alone   The man next to me watches
him through binoculars "*This* is drama"
He says it to his friend   Does he see
his life in the life of the man up above   He
is taut with anticipation   he opens his
great throat   the world is fresh and young

*

The buildings are momentary and reveal themselves
bold magnificence eked out into
this radiant strain of weather   Cameras
pass through the street   their shadows
of conscience for a moment unbearable
Then composed things appear

Acknowledgments

Grateful acknowledgment to the editors of the following publications, where some of these poems first appeared, sometimes in different versions: *Another Chicago Magazine, Caliban, Conduit, Denver Quarterly, Hayden's Ferry Review, Image, Indiana Review, The Literary Review, Passages North, Pleiades, Poet Lore, River Styx, 3rd bed, West Branch, Witness.*

Thank you to Ander Monson for publishing several of these poems in the chapbook *Beast, to Be Your Friend* (New Michigan Press, 2009). Thanks to Washington State Artist Trust and the Seattle Arts Commission. J.P. Dancing Bear, thank you for choosing this book. Thank you to my family and friends. And my eternal gratitude and love to Suzanne Bottelli—thank you for all of your support during the writing of this book, and thank you for it now.

About the Author

Jennifer Moss was born in Spokane, Washington and attended Grinnell College and the Iowa Writers' Workshop. She is the author of the chapbook *Beast, to Be Your Friend* (New Michigan Press, 2009). Her poems have appeared in *Conduit, Pleiades, Denver Quarterly, Indiana Review,* and other journals. She currently lives in Seattle.

CPSIA information can be obtained
at www.ICGtesting.com
Printed in the USA
FFOW03n2223260917
40404FF